Built for Speed

The World's Fastest Indy Cars

by Glen and Karen Bledsoe

CAPSTONE
HIGH-INTEREST
BOOKS

an imprint of Capstone Press
Mankato, Minnesota

Capstone High-Interest Books are published by Capstone Press
151 Good Counsel Drive, P.O. Box 669, Mankato, Minnesota 56002
http://www.capstone-press.com

Library of Congress Cataloging-in-Publication Data
Bledsoe, Glen.
    The world's fastest Indy cars/Glen and Karen Bledsoe.
    p. cm.—(Built for speed)
    Includes bibliographical references and index.
    Summary: Discusses the history and development of the race cars
that have been used at the Indianapolis Speedway from the early 1900s to
the present.
    ISBN 0-7368-1501-5 (hardcover)
    1. Indy cars—Juvenile literature. [1. Indy cars—History. 2. Automobiles,
Racing—History.] I. Bledsoe, Karen E. II. Title. III. Built for speed (Mankato,
Minn.) IV. Series.
TL236 .B54 2003
796.72—dc21   2002012500

Capstone Press thanks the Indianapolis Motor Speedway and the Indy Racing League for their help in preparing this book.

Editorial Credits
Matt Doeden, editor; Karen Risch, product planning editor; Timothy Halldin,
    series designer; Patrick Dentinger, book designer; Jo Miller, photo researcher

Photo Credits
Artemis Images/Indianapolis Motor Speedway, cover, 13, 14, 24;
    Ron McQueeney, 20, 22–23, 37, 47
Corbis/Bettmann, 10, 17; AFP, 32–33
Getty Images/Jamie Squire, 4, Robert Laberge, 7, 8, 18, 30, 38, 41, 44;
    Dave Sanford, 26; Robert Cianflone, 29; Brian Spurlock, 34

1 2 3 4 5 6 08 07 06 05 04 03

Table of Contents

Chapter 1

Indy Cars

More than 400,000 racing fans watch as 33 Indy car drivers slowly circle the Indianapolis Motor Speedway. The drivers follow a pace car as they prepare to begin the most famous race in the world, the Indianapolis 500.

The pace car leaves the track, and the flagman waves the green flag. All 33 drivers stomp on their accelerators as the race begins. The cars race side-by-side down the frontstretch. Engines roar as the cars reach speeds of almost 200 miles (320 kilometers) per hour. The drivers slow down as they enter the track's first turn. They move to the inside

The Indianapolis 500 is the most famous race in the world.

part of the track, then return to the outside part as they speed up again.

The cars accelerate as they exit the second turn. Several cars pull ahead of the pack as they roar down the backstretch at more than 230 miles (370 kilometers) per hour. The drivers take two more turns, then return to the starting line. They have completed the race's first 2.5-mile (4-kilometer) lap. They have 199 laps left to go.

About Indy Cars

Indy cars are highly specialized cars built just for racing. They get their name from the Indianapolis 500, but they race on many tracks around the world. Indy cars are designed to handle well at speeds of more than 200 miles (320 kilometers) per hour. They also must handle well during high-speed turns.

Indy cars belong to a class of cars called formula racers. The name "formula" refers to a set of racing rules used in some high-speed

Indy cars are built just for racing. People cannot legally drive them on streets.

races. These rules decide how cars can be built and what changes racing teams can make to a car's body and engine. Formula cars are built only for racing. People cannot legally drive them on streets.

Indy car racing is expensive. Each car costs about $300,000. Each engine can cost up to $95,000. Teams also spend a great deal of money on fuel and tires. Teams earn money to pay these costs in two ways. Each race has prize money that is divided among the drivers who take part. Teams also earn money through sponsorships. Sponsors pay race teams to promote their products. For example, an oil company may pay a team to place the company's logo on the side of a car.

Sponsors pay race teams to place company logos on their racecars.

Chapter 2

The History of Indy Cars

Indy car history began with the Indianapolis 500. For almost 100 years, this race has been the biggest and most popular car race in the world.

The Brickyard

Carl Fisher was one of the first people to imagine large race tracks for cars. In 1909, he built a track in Indianapolis. The track was a 2.5-mile (4-kilometer) rectangle. He paved the track with tar and crushed stone.

Later that year, Fisher held the first race on his track. But the track surface was not safe.

The Indianapolis Motor Speedway has held races for almost 100 years.

The track could not withstand the speed and weight of all the cars. Potholes formed all over the track. Five people died in crashes because of the poor driving surface.

Fisher knew he needed a better track surface. He made it safer by paving it with 3.2 million bricks. People began calling the track "the Brickyard." Today, the official name for the track is the Indianapolis Motor Speedway. But many people still call it the Brickyard.

Early Indy Cars

The cars in the first Indianapolis 500 races sat high off the ground and were shaped like boxes. Most of the cars were unsafe. They shook and leaked oil. The tires were of poor quality, and the brakes could not slow down the cars quickly. Both a driver and a mechanic rode in each car. They made repairs right on the track.

Over time, the cars became faster and safer. In the early 1920s, brothers Fred and Augie

The most successful early Indy cars were built by Fred and Augie Duesenberg.

Duesenberg built some of the fastest cars in the world. They worked with an engineer named Harry Miller. Miller built a powerful engine called the Miller 91. Together, Miller and the Duesenbergs helped Indy cars reach speeds of more than 150 miles (240 kilometers) per hour.

The roadster was the most popular Indy car model during the 1950s.

The Roadster

Most early Indy cars were standard street cars that had been modified for racing. The cars often looked very different from one another. This fact changed during the 1950s, when the roadster became a popular Indy car design.

Roadsters had a bullet-shaped body made of steel. Their curved front ends allowed air to easily move around the car. This aerodynamic design reduced the force of air pushing against the car as it moved. Roadsters could reach speeds of about 160 miles (260 kilometers) per hour. They handled much better than the earlier Indy car models.

Another different feature of the roadster was the placement of the engine. Engineers placed the heavy engines into the cars at an angle. The weight of this "canted" engine was mostly on the car's left side. This design helped Indy car drivers, because all of the turns on the Indianapolis Motor Speedway are to the left. The extra weight on the left side made turning easier.

Design Changes

Indy cars have changed several times since roadsters were popular. Small, narrow mid-engine cars were popular during the 1960s. People sometimes called these cars "roller skates" because of their small size and unusual shape. Mid-engine cars could reach speeds of about 150 miles (240 kilometers) per hour. Roadsters could go about 10 miles (16 kilometers) per hour faster, but mid-engine cars could take corners at much faster speeds. Mid-engine cars used less gas and did not wear out tires as quickly as roadsters did. They were also easier to drive than roadsters.

As the top speeds of Indy cars increased, car designers had a new problem. The stream of air traveling under the cars could lift them slightly off the track. This effect reduced traction. The tires could not grip the road well.

A new body style helped to solve this problem. Designers built cars very low to the ground. They also added several "wings" that caused passing air to push down on the car. This downforce helped the car's tires stay on the track. Wings are still an important part of Indy car designs.

The modern design of Indy cars started during the late 1960s and early 1970s.

Chapter 3

Indy Car Design

Today's Indy cars can reach speeds of more than 240 miles (385 kilometers) per hour on long tracks. Every part of an Indy car is designed for racing. These designs allow modern Indy cars to be safe as well as fast.

The Engine

A powerful engine is the most important part of an Indy car. Indy cars have internal combustion engines. These engines burn fuel inside a set of eight cylinders. The burning causes pistons inside the cylinders to quickly pump up and down. This motion powers the car.

Indy car engines burn a fuel called methanol. This alcohol-based fuel gives

---

Today, Indy cars can reach speeds of more than 240 miles (385 kilometers) per hour.

The body of an Indy car is made of shaped panels.

engines a great deal of power. Most Indy cars
go only about 2 miles (3.2 kilometers) on each
gallon of fuel they burn. They have a large
35-gallon (132-liter) tank to make up for this
poor fuel mileage.

Indy car engines can produce up to
700 horsepower. Standard street cars
produce only about 150 horsepower. With

these powerful engines, Indy cars can reach speeds of 60 miles (97 kilometers) per hour in only 2 seconds. They can reach 100 miles (160 kilometers) per hour in about 4 seconds.

The Body

The metal frame of an Indy car is called the chassis. All of the car's other parts connect to the chassis. The body of the car is made of shaped panels. The panels are made of fiberglass, aluminum, carbon fiber, and other strong, lightweight materials.

Racing leagues control the size of Indy cars. In the Indy Racing League (IRL), the body must be between 192 and 196 inches (488 and 498 centimeters) long and no more than 78.5 inches (200 centimeters) wide. It must stand about 38 inches (97 centimeters) tall. An Indy car must weigh at least 1,550 pounds (703 kilograms). These size rules help league officials make sure all of the cars in a race are about equal in performance.

Smooth tires called slicks give Indy cars a good grip on paved tracks.

Tires and Brakes

Indy cars use smooth tires called slicks. Slicks grip paved surfaces very well. This grip improves an Indy car's acceleration and speed.

Racing teams change tires several times during a race. Slicks wear down quickly at high speeds. Drivers must make pit stops so team members can put new tires on the car. Each set of four tires costs about $1,200. Teams may use 10 or more sets during a race.

Tires fit over cast magnesium wheels. These metal wheels are 15 inches (38 centimeters) in diameter. They are usually 10 to 14 inches (25 to 36 centimeters) wide.

Indy cars need powerful brakes to slow down. Each wheel is fitted with a carbon disc brake. Clamps called calipers squeeze the discs to slow the wheels. The pressure of the squeezing calipers makes the discs red hot. Standard metal disc brakes would fall apart from this heat. Carbon discs withstand the heat better.

Safety

Indy car builders try to design the safest cars possible. A car moving at more than 200 miles (320 kilometers) per hour has a great deal of energy. The force of a crash into a wall can kill a driver. Indy cars are built to break apart during a crash. Much of the car's energy is used up as it breaks apart. The driver does not have to withstand as much of the energy on impact. This design cannot completely protect drivers, but it does help during many crashes.

Leagues also have safety teams at every race. These teams include doctors, firefighters, rescue specialists, and paramedics. Rescue teams are ready to hurry onto the track at any time. Each track also has its own medical center. An ambulance is always ready to rush anyone with a serious injury to a hospital.

Drivers wear helmets with full face shields.

Chapter 4

Indy Car Races

Two organizations run most of the major Indy car races in North America. They are the Indy Racing League (IRL) and Championship Auto Racing Teams (CART). Each racing league has its own set of rules and races. But some drivers take part in races for both leagues.

Tracks

Indy cars race on many types of tracks, including speedways, road courses, and street courses. Speedways, such as the Indianapolis Motor Speedway, are long, oval tracks. They have two long, straight areas called straightaways. One straightaway,

Road courses are curving tracks built just for racing.

called the frontstretch, includes the start and finish line. The other straightaway is called the backstretch.

Road courses are curving tracks built just for racing. They often include hills, S-shaped turns, and sharp hairpin turns. Road courses rarely have long straightaways.

Street courses are race tracks set up on city streets. Race officials block off sections of streets to form street courses. They prevent normal traffic from entering the course. Street courses often have very sharp corners and few long straightaways.

Before a Race

Qualifying is the first part of every Indy car race. Each driver takes a qualifying run to decide the starting order of the race. Qualifying runs are also called time trials. Race officials time each driver's qualifying laps. The driver with the fastest lap earns the pole position and begins the race on the inside part of the first row. The second fastest driver

Street courses are set up on blocked-off city streets.

begins the race on the outside position of the first row. The remaining drivers line up on the starting grid according to their times.

Race officials carefully inspect each car before a race. They make sure the racing team has followed all league rules. They measure the car to make sure the car meets all of the league's size and weight rules. They check the size of the gas tank. They also make sure the car is safe for racing.

The Race

The drivers take several warm-up laps behind a pace car after they line up on the starting grid. When the pace car leaves the track, a flagman waves a green flag to begin the race. The drivers quickly accelerate and try to pass one another.

The flagman may wave a yellow caution flag if there is a crash during the race. The pace car then returns to the track. Drivers line up behind the pace car again. They may not

Drivers may pass each other at any time when a green flag is waving.

A pit crew changes the car's tires, adds fuel, and makes other needed repairs.

pass one another until the track is clear and the flagman waves the green flag again.

Cars need to make pit stops for fuel and tires. To make pit stops, drivers pull the car into the pit area. A team of skilled mechanics called a pit crew then works on the car. The pit crew changes the car's tires, adds fuel,

and makes any other needed repairs. The crew
also gives the driver a drink. A good pit crew
can complete all of these tasks in about
10 seconds.

The flagman waves a white flag when the
leader has one more lap to complete. He waves
a checkered flag as the winning driver crosses
the finish line.

Chapter 5

Indy Car Stars

Indy car racing is one of the most popular motor sports in North America. Millions of fans attend IRL and CART races each year.

Some of the most famous drivers in racing history have driven Indy cars. Early stars such as Tommy Milton, Lou Meyer, and Wilbur Shaw first interested people in Indy cars. In the 1960s and 1970s, A. J. Foyt, Al Unser, and other stars made Indy racing famous worldwide. In the 1980s and early 1990s, Emerson Fittipaldi, Rick Mears, and Al Unser Jr. were among the most popular drivers. Today, fan favorites include Sam Hornish Jr., Michael Andretti, and Helio Castroneves.

A. J. Foyt was one of the biggest Indy car stars during the 1960s and 1970s.

Sam Hornish Jr.

Many racing experts consider Sam Hornish Jr. to be one of the best young drivers in auto racing. As a teenager, Hornish was a champion go-kart racer. In 2000, he began racing in the IRL at age 19. He finished in the top 10 of two races that year and finished fourth in the Rookie of the Year standings.

Hornish won three races in 2001, including the season's first two races. He easily won the IRL championship and became the youngest Indy car champion in history.

Hornish started another successful season in 2002 by winning two of the first three IRL races. With two races to go, he and several other drivers were in a close battle for the championship. Hornish won the Delphi Indy 300 by .0024 of a second, the closest margin in IRL history. He then won the last race, the Chevy 500, to earn his second straight IRL championship.

Sam Hornish Jr. won IRL titles in 2001 and 2002.

Michael Andretti

Michael Andretti comes from a racing family. His father, Mario, is one of the biggest Indy car stars in history. His brother Jeff also races Indy cars. His cousin John is a driver in NASCAR's Winston Cup Series.

Andretti started his career as a go-kart driver. He won 50 of the 75 go-kart races he entered between 1972 and 1979. He later moved to Indy car racing. In 1984, he qualified fourth in his first Indianapolis 500. In 1991, he won CART's FedEx Championship Series. He has also finished second in the championship standings five times. He has won more CART races than any driver in the league's history. In 2002, Andretti announced that he was leaving CART to drive in the IRL.

Andretti has won more than 40 Indy car races during his career. Only his father and racing legend A. J. Foyt have won more races.

Michael Andretti has won more than 40 Indy car races during his career.

Helio Castroneves

Helio Castroneves has been a star in both CART and the IRL. Like Hornish and Andretti, Castroneves began his racing career in go-karts. In 1989, he won the Brazilian National Go-Kart Championship.

Castroneves began racing in CART in 1998. He did not win any races during his first two years, but he finished second twice. Castroneves became a star in 2000, when he won three CART races and finished seventh in the FedEx Championship Series. In 2001, Castroneves again won three CART races. He finished fourth in the FedEx Championship Series. He also won the IRL's Indianapolis 500.

In 2002, Castroneves left CART to join the IRL. There, he won two of his first five races, including the Indianapolis 500. He finished second to Hornish by only 20 points in the IRL championship.

Helio Castroneves has been a star in both CART and the IRL.

Words to Know

aerodynamic (air-oh-dye-NAM-mik)—designed to reduce air resistance

chassis (CHASS-ee)—the central body of an Indy car, including the driver's compartment

cylinder (SIL-uhn-dur)—a hollow tube inside which a piston moves up and down to produce power in an engine

methanol (METH-uh-nawl)—an alcohol-based fuel used by Indy cars

modify (MOD-uh-fye)—to change; mechanics modify the engine and body of an Indy car to improve its performance.

slicks (SLIKS)—soft tires that have no tread

traction (TRAK-shuhn)—the grip of a car's tires on the ground

To Learn More

Fish, Bruce. *Indy Car Racing.* Race Car Legends. Philadelphia: Chelsea House, 2001.

McKenna, A. T. *Indy Racing.* Fast Tracks. Edina, Minn.: Adbo & Daughters, 1998.

Sessler, Peter and Nilda. *Indy Cars.* Off to the Races. Vero Beach, Fla.: Rourke Press, 1999.

Useful Addresses

Championship Auto Racing Teams (CART)
5350 Lakeview Parkway South Drive
Building 36
Inner Park/Park 100
Indianapolis, IN 46268

Indianapolis Motor Speedway
4790 West 16th Street
Indianapolis, IN 46222

Indy Racing League (IRL)
4565 West 16th Street
Indianapolis, IN 46222

Internet Sites

Do you want to learn more about Indy cars?
Visit the FACT HOUND at *http://www.facthound.com*

FACT HOUND can track down many sites to help you.
All the FACT HOUND sites are hand-selected by Capstone
Press editors. FACT HOUND will fetch the best, most accurate
information to answer your questions.

IT IS EASY! IT IS FUN!
1) Go to *http://www.facthound.com*
2) Type in: 0736815015
3) Click on "FETCH IT" and FACT HOUND will put you on
the trail of several helpful links.

**You can also search by subject or book title. So, relax
and let our pal FACT HOUND do the research for you!**

Index